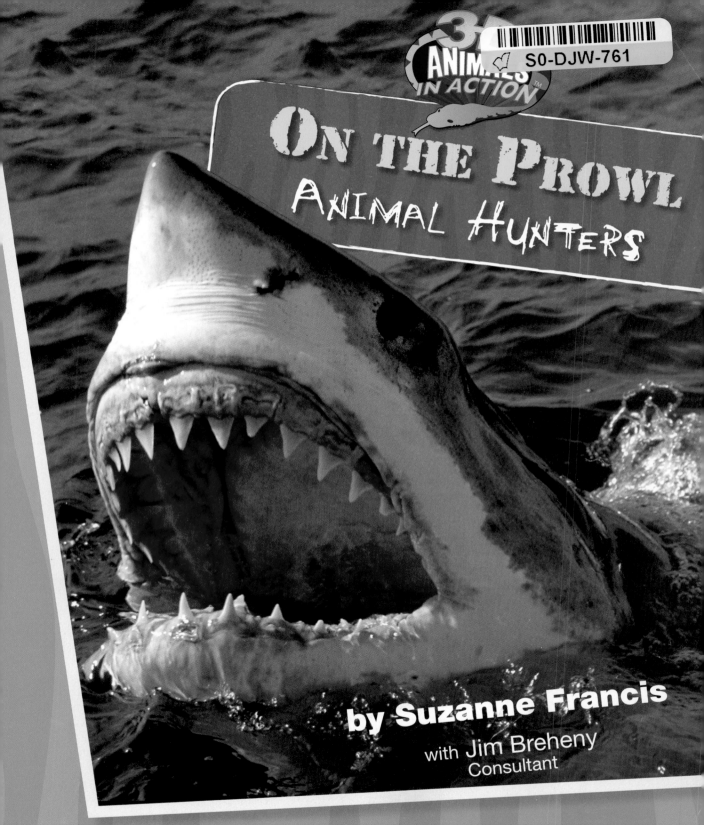

3D ANIMALS IN ACTION™

ON THE PROWL
ANIMAL HUNTERS

by Suzanne Francis

with Jim Breheny
Consultant

Scholastic Inc.

New York • Toronto • London • Auckland • Sydney
Mexico City • New Delhi • Hong Kong • Buenos Aires

ISBN-13: 978-0-439-02575-1
ISBN-10: 0-439-02575-3

Design by Aruna Goldstein
All Mac the veiled chameleon illustrations by James Elston

Photo Credits:
Cover: (Shark) © Doug Perrine/SeaPics.com. Back cover: (Leopard) © Tim Davis/Stone/Getty Images. Pages 4–5: (Young green tree python) © Frank Lane Picture Agency/CORBIS. Pages 6–7: (Cheetah with prey) © Anup Shah/Riser/Getty Images; (vultures) © William Manning/CORBIS. Pages 8–9: (Leaping shark) © Amos Nachoum/The Image Bank/Getty Images; (sand tiger shark) © Jeff Rotman/Iconica/Getty Images. Pages 10–11: (Shark egg case) © Alexis Rosenfeld/Photo Researchers, Inc.; (shark school) © Steve Drogin/SeaPics.com; (great white shark) © Stephen Frink/Science Faction/Getty Images; (hammerhead shark) © Masa Ushioda/SeaPics.com. Pages 12–13: (Roaring lion) © Renee Lynn/Stone/Getty Images; (tiger) © Tom Brakefield/CORBIS. Pages 14–15: (Lion pride) © Art Wolfe/Photo Researchers, Inc.; (leopard) © Mike Hill/Photographer's Choice RR/Getty Images; (cheetah) © Theo Allofs/Photonica/Getty Images. Pages 16–17: (Gyrfalcon) © James Balog/Aurora/Getty Images; (bald eagle with fish) © Johnny Johnson/The Image Bank/Getty Images. Pages 18–19: (Red-tailed hawk) © Jeffrey Lepore/Photo Researchers, Inc.; (African white-backed vulture) © Nigel J. Dennis/Photo Researchers, Inc.; (bald eagle) © Thomas & Pat Leeson/Photo Researchers, Inc.; (peregrine falcon) © Ann & Steve Toon/Photo Researchers, Inc.; (Philippine eagle) © Daniel Heuclin/Photo Researchers, Inc. Pages 20–21: (Dwarf crocodile) © Martin Harvey/Photo Researchers, Inc.; (alligator with fish) © Luis Castaneda Inc/The Image Bank/Getty Images. Pages 22–23: (Crocodile with baby) © Anup Shah/The Image Bank/Getty Images; (gharial) © Aaron Ferster/Photo Researchers, Inc.; (American alligator) © Ron Levine/Photographer's Choice/Getty Images. Pages 24–25: (Carpet python with lizard) © Oliver Strewe/Stone/Getty Images; (emerald tree boa) © E. R. Degginger/Photo Researchers, Inc.; (anaconda) © Ed George/National Geographic/Getty Images. Pages 26–27: (Piranha teeth) © Dr. Paul A. Zahl/Photo Researchers, Inc.; (piranha) © Reinhard Dirscherl/SeaPics.com; (archerfish) © Stephen Dalton/Photo Researchers, Inc. Pages 28–29: (Fossa) © Nick Garbutt/Photo Researchers, Inc.; (African wild dogs) © Ann & Steve Toon/Photo Researchers, Inc. Page 30: (Alligator snapping turtle) © George Grall/National Geographic/Getty Images. Page 31: (Hans Walters) © Julie Larsen Maher/WCS. Page 32: (Shark) © Kike Calvo/V & W/SeaPics.com.

12 11 10 9 8 7 6 5 4 3 2 1   7 8 9 10 11 12/0

Printed in the U.S.A.

First Scholastic printing, July 2007

TABLE OF CONTENTS

WELCOME TO ANIMAL HUNTERS!

Mac
Veiled chameleon

Hi there, explorer! It's your best chameleon buddy, Mac! Are you up for a power-packed adventure? We're prowling around the exciting world of animal hunters. We'll meet some of the fiercest, fastest, and most fascinating animals around. Did you know that…

* A SHARK CAN SNIFF OUT A SINGLE DROP OF BLOOD IN OVER 16,000 GALLONS OF WATER?

* BALD EAGLES CAN BUILD NESTS THAT ARE AS BIG AS CARS?

* SOME REPTILE MOMS TOTE THEIR TOTS AROUND IN THEIR JAWS?

And we'll find out the answers to questions like…

* WHY DO TIGERS HAVE STRIPES?

* WHAT'S THE DIFFERENCE BETWEEN AN ALLIGATOR AND A CROCODILE?

* HOW MANY TEETH DOES A GREAT WHITE SHARK HAVE?

Whenever you see this icon, make sure you slap on your **3-D glasses** to see these pictures come to life!

▶ A python hangs out on a branch.

READY TO START OUR ADVENTURE?
TURN THE PAGE AND LET'S MAKE SOME TRACKS!

ON THE HUNT

nimal hunters are predators that find, catch, and kill other animals for food. They're **carnivores** (KAR-nuh-vors), so they want one thing: meat! Check out these pages to get the scoop on what hunters need to make the catch of the day.

The Word Bird

A *carnivore* is an animal that only eats meat.

Cheetah with prey

A group of vultures

MAKes Sense to Me

Before they can catch prey, hunters need to find it! Luckily, most hunters have some super-senses to help them out. Some hunters have **amazing eyesight and hearing** to help them spot prey. Others just follow their noses! Some predators count on their **outstanding sniffers** to track down prey.

Take A Bite

Hunters aren't in the mood for milk shakes—they need meat! So these animals need a **good set of chompers** or **sharp beaks** to kill and eat prey. Some hunters use their teeth to rip off large chunks of food that they swallow right down. No chewing!

On the Run

Some animal hunters can **zoom at high speeds** since the prey they're chasing is seriously fast food. Other hunters can only **move fast for short distances**. They hide and have to **sneak up on prey** before they make their move.

Go Team!

Most hunters, like the great white shark or the tiger, hunt alone. But some hunters like a little company. Lions and African wild dogs **team up and hunt in groups**. Even though they have to share their food later, these animals can take down large prey and help protect each other at the same time.

SHOW ME SOME FIN

Our first group of animal hunters has prowled the rivers and oceans of Earth for 350 million years. They're **sharks**! Read on to get the scoop on these ancient hunters.

▶ A shark leaps up to snatch a meal.

✴ Sharks are **cartilaginous** (KAR-tuh-LAH-jin-uhss) fish, which means that their skeletons are made of **cartilage** (KAR-tuh-lij), not bone. They usually have long bodies and powerful tails that help them swim.

✴ Sharks breathe through slits on the sides of their heads called **gills**. Some sharks need to constantly swim to move water over them, but others can pump water over their gills when they're lying still.

✴ Shark skin is made up of tiny, overlapping plates called **denticles** (DEN-tih-kuhls). These denticles help protect the sharks and make their skin feel very rough, like sandpaper.

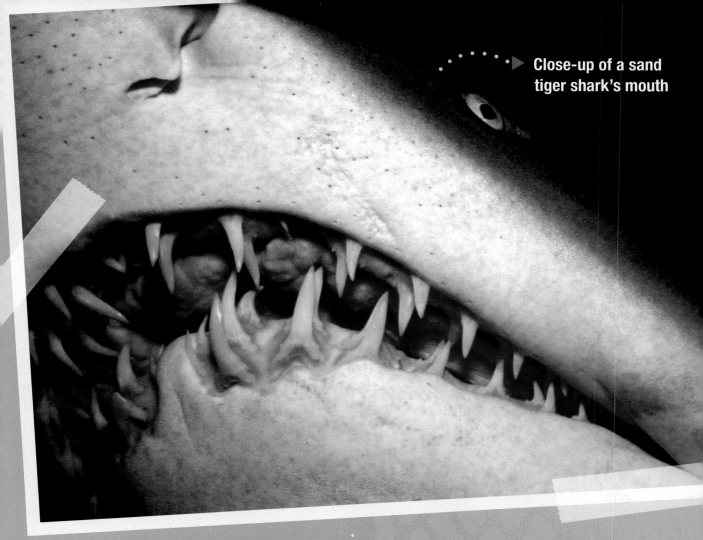

Close-up of a sand tiger shark's mouth

The Nose Knows

A shark's nose only has one job—to sniff out prey. Some sharks can smell a single drop of blood in a billion drops of water—that's over 16,000 gallons (60,567 l)! Along with its super sense of smell, sharks have **tiny openings in their skin that sense small amounts of electricity** that all animals give off. Sharks can sense prey even when it's hiding deep in the sand on the seafloor.

Sharky Smile

If you look inside a shark's mouth, you'd see that it has **extra rows of teeth** behind its front ones. Why so toothy? A shark bites down and shakes its head to kill and eat prey. This is pretty tough on the shark's teeth, so if one breaks or falls out, **another tooth from the next row moves forward to take its place.** This helps the shark keep a mouthful of teeth ready for major meat-eating. Some sharks lose as many as 30,000 teeth during their lifetime!

that's **Wild!**

An adult whale shark grows up to 50 feet (15 m) long, making it the biggest fish in the world.

Fin Frenzy

Most sharks aren't picky eaters. They'll eat all sorts of things, like seals, stingrays, turtles, shrimp, and crabs. They'll also eat dead animals and some will even eat garbage! While sharks like to hunt alone, other sharks can smell the blood in the water after one makes a catch. And if a bunch show up, one shark's meal can turn into a feeding frenzy. The sharks will bite at anything they can get their jaws around—even each other!

Shark egg case

that's Wild! All sharks make eggs. Some sharks hatch eggs inside their bodies so that their babies are born live. Other sharks lay eggs in leathery cases with stringy hooks to attach it to seaweed or rocks.

A school of sharks

Now that you've scoped out these awesome hunters, take a bite out of the two super sharks below!

Hammerhead Shark

Size: Up to 11½ feet (3½ m) long
Location: Warm, tropical waters all over the world

As you might have guessed, the **hammerhead shark** has a wide, thick head that looks like a hammer. The eyes on a great hammerhead can be as far apart as 3 feet (1 m)! Most sharks like to swim alone, but hammerheads swim in schools. These sharks love to eat stingrays and use their heads to pin them down while biting their wings.

Great White Shark

Size: Up to 20 feet (6 m) long
Location: Coastlines all over the world

Great white sharks have extremely powerful jaws and lots of sharp, triangular teeth—around 3,000! They also have the biggest shark teeth around—up to 3 inches (8 cm) long. Great whites eat seals, dolphins, sea turtles, and dead animals. They can rip off a chunk of flesh that weighs as much as 20 pounds (9 kg)!

FEAR FACTOR

Many people fear sharks because they think they attack humans, but sharks don't go out looking for people. More people die from beestings than from shark attacks! People are a bigger threat to sharks—at least 40 million are killed every year to make shark fin soup. Many people are trying to make shark hunting illegal so these predators don't become extinct.

FELINE FINE

Roaring male lion

Now let's meet some furry, four-legged land hunters—and they're grrrreat! Read on to learn more about the **big cats.**

★ Big cats like lions, tigers, and leopards are meat-eating **mammals** (MAM-uhls) and belong to the same group as house cats.

★ Big cats have 28–30 teeth that can cut through bone. Their **canine** (KAY-nine) **teeth** are larger than any other carnivore's. Their smaller front teeth help strip away skin and tear meat.

★ Most big cats have **long, super-sharp claws** that help the cat grab and hold on to prey. The claws are also **retractable**. They draw back into their toes when they're not being used so that the tips stay nice and sharp.

The Word Bird

Mammals are furry, warm-blooded animals whose bodies make milk for their young. *Canine teeth* are the long, pointed teeth in animals like cats and dogs. They're also called *fangs*.

Stripes are paw-some!

Tiger

TOP TIGERS

The **tiger** is the biggest and most powerful cat in the world and makes its home in the forests and grasslands of South and East Asia. These big cats can measure up to 10½ feet (3 m) long and weigh around 700 pounds (318 kg). Tigers hunt solo and kill prey with a deadly bite to the back of the neck or by crushing the prey's throat. While they're famous for their big and bold stripes, a tiger's coloring actually helps it to hide. The stripes blend the tiger into the shadows and make it hard to see where its body begins and ends.

that's WILD! Most big cats hate water, but not tigers! During hot days, tigers hang out in water to keep cool. Some tigers that live on islands can even swim to other islands.

Lion pride

That's a **king-sized** meal!

MAne MAMMAL

You might know our second cat as the king of the jungle. But unlike tigers, these cats aren't loners— they like a little company! **Lions** live and hunt in groups called *prides*. Female lions usually form groups of 4–6 related adults, including one or two males, and hunt and raise their young together. Male lions have thick manes of fur on their heads and neck, but females don't have this heavy fur collar. Lions don't hunt or eat every day and may go several days or even a week without eating. But when they do, they eat a lot! A male lion can eat up to 75 pounds (34 kg) in one meal!

that's WILD!

A lion's roar is no meow. It can be heard up to 5 miles (8 km) away!

Seeing Spots

Leopards live in Asia and Africa and they can grow up to 6 feet (2 m) long and weigh up to 150 pounds (68 kg). These big cats have a serious case of spots, called **rosettes** (ROH-sehts), that go right down to their skin. Leopards love hanging out, taking naps, and eating meals high up in a tree or hidden in a thick bush. They can catch large prey and drag it into a tree to hide it from other predators. In fact, leopards can climb as high as 50 feet (15 m) with a dead animal in their mouths!

► Leopard

Cheetah

Fast Feline

The **cheetah** has an amazing claim to fame: It's the world's fastest land animal! It can catch speeds up to 70 miles (113 km) per hour! Found in Africa and South Asia, cheetahs are the only member of the cat family that don't have retractable claws. Having claws out all the time gives them an extra grip on the ground and helps them to run faster. Cheetahs don't have too much trouble catching up to prey, but other predators often come and snatch their meals!

SKY HIGH

Our next group of hunters lives nearly all over the world and rules the skies. **Raptors** (RAP-turs) are hunting birds like eagles, owls, vultures, hawks, and falcons. Read on to get the scoop on what makes these hunters truly terrific!

* Raptors have some **sharp senses** to spot prey while they're high up in the air. Scientists think that their eyesight is about four times better than yours and they have incredible hearing, too.

* A raptor has a **hooked beak** with sharp edges for eating prey. Some raptors swallow prey whole—bones and all. Or they use their sharp beaks to rip off bite-sized pieces. Yum!

* Raptors use their **powerful feet and legs** to catch and hold prey. Their feet also have sharp, curved claws called **talons** that they use to kill animals.

Gyrfalcon

Snacking Styles

Although hawks and falcons are both birds of prey, they hunt a little differently. When a hawk spots a tasty critter on the ground, it swoops down and snatches it up with its feet. Then the hawk uses its powerful toes and sharp claws to squeeze and kill the prey. Falcons, on the other hand, feed mostly on smaller birds and catch their meals high in the air. When they see something delicious, they dive at speeds of up to 200 miles (322 km) per hour and slam into it feet-first. Then they use their beaks to bite the prey on the neck to kill it.

A bald eagle catches a fish in its talons.

Critter Crack-Ups

Q: Why is it easy for a raptor to catch prey?
A: Because it's *talon*-ted.

It's time to hit the skies and check out these awesome raptors!

Red-tailed Hawk

Size: Body up to 23 inches (58 cm) long, wingspan up to 4 feet (1 m) wide
Location: North America

Like other raptors, **red-tailed hawks** have incredible eyesight and can spot a mouse from 100 feet (30½ m) away! These birds of prey can make themselves at home everywhere, from the city to the country. A famous red-tailed hawk named Pale Male built a nest with his mate on Fifth Avenue in New York City in 1991. Talk about a city slicker!

Bald Eagle

Size: Body up to 3 feet (1 m) long, wingspan up to 7 feet (2 m) wide
Location: North America

Bald eagles are great hunters with sharp eyesight and amazing flying power. These birds can catch speeds up to 100 miles (161 km) per hour when diving! And these raptors like to live large—their massive nests can be 10 feet (3 m) across. That's bigger than a car! Bald eagles eat mostly fish, but also hunt small mammals, snakes, and other birds.

Peregrine Falcon

Size: Up to 15 inches (38 cm) long
Location: Worldwide, except Antarctica

The **peregrine falcon** is the fastest flying bird around. It can zip through the air and dive to catch prey at speeds up to 200 miles (322 km) per hour! These raptors hunt during the day and eat mostly birds, like pigeons and ducks.

Philippine Eagle

Size: Up to 3 feet (1 m) long, wingspan 7 feet (2 m) wide
Location: Rain forests of the Philippines

One of the rarest raptors around, the **Philippine eagle** is famous for chowing down on monkeys, medium-sized mammals, lizards, and large birds. Its head has a mane of long brown feathers that puffs up when it feels threatened.

African White-backed Vulture

Size: Body up to 3 feet (1 m) long, wingspan up to 11 feet (3 m) wide
Location: Africa

African white-backed vultures are **scavengers** (SKAV-en-jers) with large, broad wings that help them fly high for hours and look for dead animals that they can chow down on. These birds also have a long neck covered with downy fuzz. Unlike other birds of prey, vultures like to hang out in groups and keep an eye on each other. If one bird spots something tasty and dives for it, the others follow since it's a sure sign of lunch!

The Word Bird

A *scavenger* is an animal that feeds on plants or animals that are already dead.

Crocs Rock

Our next group of animals is packed with big-mouthed predators who hunt and hang out on both land and water—**crocodilians** (CROK-oh-DILL-ee-uns). What makes these crazy crocs tick? Check it out!

- Crocodilians are **reptiles**, so they're **cold-blooded** creatures, like snakes and lizards. Their body temperature depends on their surroundings, so these animals warm up by hanging out in the sun and cool down by slipping into the water.
- Crocodilians **spend most of their time in water** and are super swimmers. Their **eyes and nostrils are on the tops of their heads** so that they can still breathe and see when the rest of their bodies are underwater.
- A crocodilian's body is covered in **large, bony scales** called **scutes** (SKYOOTS). Their skin sheds in chunks as they grow or as it wears out.

Dwarf crocodile

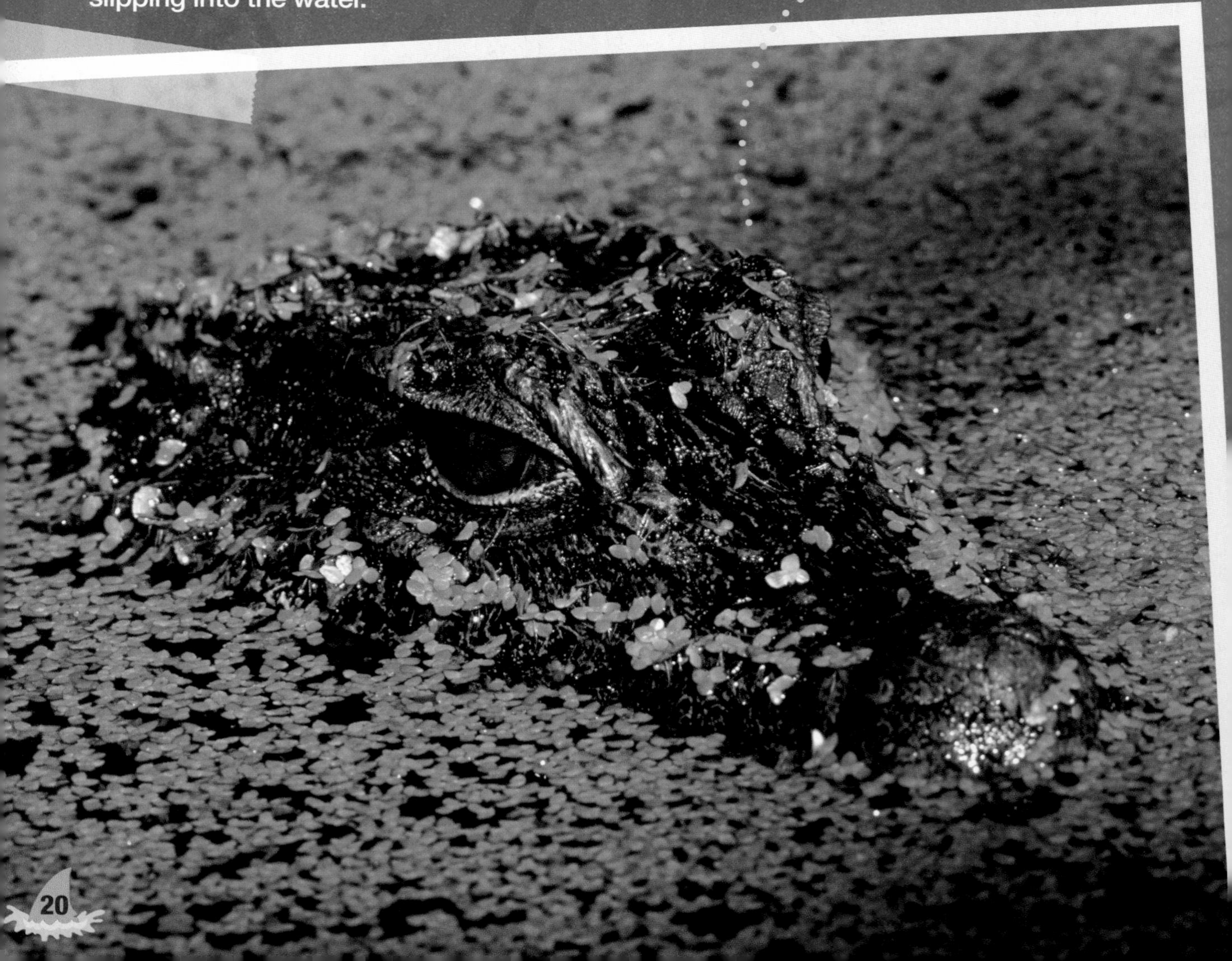

▶ An alligator bites down on a fish.

A NASTY SURPRISE

Crocodilians aren't the fastest creatures around, but they're still expert predators. They're **ambush** hunters, which means they **hide and surprise their prey**. Since their eyes and nostrils are on top of their heads and snouts, crocodilians can hide underwater for hours. Once they see a tasty morsel, a crocodilian grabs it in its jaws and clamps down. Some crocodilians can jump up to 5 feet (1½ m) in the air to snatch birds or bats.

JUMBO JAWS

Crocodilians have **powerful jaws** for biting and killing prey. They can snap right through a turtle's shell or crush the leg bones of a buffalo. But crocodilian jaws **aren't made for chewing**. After they catch their prey, crocs stick it underwater for a bit to soften up, or grab it with their jaws and spin around until a chunk rips off.

A crocodile carries her baby to water.

Croc babies **ride** in style!

ROCK-A-BYE REPTILE

Even though they're fierce predators, crocodilians are one of the few kinds of reptiles that take care of their young. After the croc mom digs her nest and lays her eggs, she hangs around and protects them from predators until they hatch. Once they do, the mom opens her mouth and carries them to water in her jumbo jaws. Many young crocs stay near their mothers for up to three years.

that's Wild!

Did you know that some alligators can survive in icy waters? When the water freezes, their bodies are trapped in ice, but as long as their nostrils stick out, they can still breathe.

CROC OR GATOR?

The crocodilian group includes both crocodiles and alligators. But how do you tell them apart? Crocodiles have pointy V-shaped snouts. Alligator snouts are flatter, wider, and more U-shaped. Also, the fourth tooth on the lower jaw of a crocodile sticks up over its upper lip. Crocodiles also have special glands that let them live in saltwater. Alligators don't, so they stay near freshwater areas.

Critter Crack-Ups

Q: Why can't the alligator make a phone call?
A: Because it can't *croco*-dial!

school of croc

Now that you've rocked with crocs, it's time to whoop it up with two super-cool crocodilians.

Gharial

Size: Up to 23 feet (7 m) long
Location: Nepal, Pakistan, India, and southern Asia

A **gharial** (guh-REE-uhl) is a crocodilian with a long, skinny snout that makes it a great swimmer. And that's good because this croc only craves one thing: fish! Its super-long jaws are lined with over 100 needle-like teeth that are perfect for nabbing a slippery fish. This croc is named for the bump on the end of a male's snout, since "ghara" is the Hindi word for "mud pot."

American Alligator

Size: Up to 18 feet (6 m) long
Location: Southeastern United States

The **American alligator** is the largest reptile in North America and lives in warm swamps, rivers, and lakes. These gators are slow-moving animals on land, but they can sprint for short distances at speeds of up to 30 miles (48 km) per hour. Alligators will eat just about anything including fish, birds, mammals—even cats and dogs!

A TIGHT SQUEEZE

Our next group of hunters likes to give their prey a hug before they eat it! **Boas** and **pythons** are types of snakes that live in the rain forests of Australia, Asia, South America, and Africa. How do these armless and legless hunters catch their meals? Read on and find out.

A carpet python constricts a lizard.

HUGS OF DEATH

Boas and pythons are part of a group of snakes called **constrictors** (kuhn-STRIK-turs). These snakes don't use toxic venom to catch a meal. Instead, they **wrap themselves around prey and squeeze**. Every time their prey breathes out, these snakes squeeze tighter, until the prey can't breathe at all! Once the animal is dead, these snakes swallow their prey whole. They can even gulp down meals way bigger than they are!

In the pits

Boas and pythons hide and get very close to prey before striking. Some snakes have special holes around their noses and mouths called **heat pits** that help them find prey, even in the dark. These heat pits **sense tiny changes in temperature**. So, if a mouse scurries by at night, these snakes feel its body heat and strike!

main squeeze

Get the scoop on these two superb snakes.

Emerald Tree Boa

Size: Up to 6½ feet (2 m) long
Location: Northern South America

The **emerald tree boa** lives in the rain forests of South America where it hangs out in trees and waits for a meal. This snake has large teeth to grab prey and hang on while it constricts. Its green color is perfect for blending into rain forest leaves, but these snakes aren't born that way! Baby emerald boas are born yellow or red and don't turn green for about a year.

Anaconda

Size: Up to 20 feet (6 m) long
Location: Northern South America

The **anaconda** is a whopper of a constrictor—at a record 550 pounds (249 kg), it's the world's heaviest snake, and can grow as long as a pick-up truck! This super-sized snake lives mostly in shallow water where it hides and waits for large prey, like deer, to take a drink. Then the anaconda surprises the prey, squeezes it to death, and snacks on.

MORE MEAT-EATERS

The animals that you'll meet in this chapter might not look like fierce hunters, but they really are. Read on and meet the other members of the carnivore club!

Eaten Alive!

Our next hunter likes its food fresh—it eats its prey alive! **Piranhas** (puh-RAN-uhs) are carnivorous fish that swim in schools in the fresh waters of South America. Their most extreme feature is their lower jaw filled with small, super-sharp teeth. And piranhas definitely use 'em! These fish will nibble on any prey in their reach, usually an animal coming for a dip. A school of piranha can strip an animal of its flesh within minutes!

Close-up of a piranha's teeth

That's major munchies!

Piranha

An archerfish shoots an insect.

SHARP SHOOTER

Archerfish are small critters about 5 inches (13 cm) long that swim in waters around India, the Philippines, Australia, and Polynesia. These fish have an amazing secret weapon to catch prey. Using their super-sharp eyesight, they can spot prey above them and spit a jet of water—like a water gun! Once the water jet hits the prey, it falls down and the archerfish gulps it up. Archerfish have great aim, too—they almost never miss. This fish can hit insects 6 feet (2 m) above the water's surface!

F is for Fierce

Would you believe that the world's most ferocious hunter is less than 3 feet (1 m) long? **Fossas** (FOO-sas) are meat-eating mammals only found in rain forests on the island of Madagascar. Their curved, retractable claws help them climb trees and their muscular bodies let them jump from tree to tree like squirrels! They eat small animals like rodents and reptiles, but fossas are famous for hunting lemurs, which are no easy catch!

Scientists studying lemurs first figured out that there was a fierce hunter on the prowl when animals they were studying would just disappear!

 **that's WILD!** A fossa looks like a cross between a dog and a cat, but it's not related to either. Its closest relative is a small mammal called a mongoose.

▶ **Fossa**

African wild dogs

Doggone It!

African wild dogs live in Africa and are also called **painted dogs** because of the spotted patterns on their fur. These dogs grow up to 30 inches (76 cm) high and hunt large animals like antelope and wildebeests in packs of 10–15 dogs. By hunting in packs, African wild dogs can catch just about anything! They'll chase an animal until it's totally worn out and can't run anymore. They might chase prey as far as 3 miles (5 km)!

That's one wild **dog** chase!

An alligator snapping turtle shows its pink tongue lure.

Oh, SNAP!

You might be surprised to hear that a turtle is a great hunter, but this one is no joke! The **alligator snapping turtle** lives in freshwater lakes and rivers of North America and can grow to be 4 feet (1 m) long and weigh over 200 pounds (91 kg). It has a thick shell covered in pointy plates to protect it from predators. The strangest thing about this turtle is that the tip of its tongue looks like a worm. While it's underwater, the turtle opens up and wiggles its tongue to attract fish looking for a tasty snack. Once they get close, the turtle snaps its powerful jaws shut and gulps its meal down.

Q & A WITH MARINE BIOLOGIST
HANS WALTERS

Hans with a shark

Meet Hans Walters, a marine biologist at the New York Aquarium. Hans helps care for many different kinds of animals on exhibit at the aquarium and is an expert on sharks. We got to ask Hans a few questions on these awesome predators.

Q: How did you get into studying sharks?

A: I've been interested in sharks since I was very young, and I studied marine biology in college so I could work with them full-time. My job at the New York Aquarium lets me study the sharks that live there, and I study sharks in the wild, too.

Q: What's your favorite shark and why?

A: I would have to choose the sand tiger shark. It's the one that I know the most about since we have them here at the aquarium, and I study them in the wild. This shark looks scary, but it's really an easygoing animal. Unfortunately, this shark is threatened in the wild, which is one major reason I'm studying them.

Q: Do you swim with sharks? Isn't it scary?

A: I only swim with sharks for research, or to do work in their tank at the aquarium. At first it was a little scary, but the sharks I work with, like sand tigers and nurse sharks, don't usually bother humans. I've also learned how to act so I don't make the sharks feel threatened or afraid. But they're large animals with sharp teeth, so I'm always careful.

Q: What do you think is the coolest thing about sharks?

A: That's a hard question, since there's so much to choose from! I would have to say that it's fascinating how many different kinds of sharks are out there. There are sharks that live in freshwater, as well as ones that live in saltwater. Some sharks live in very cold polar regions, while others live in warm, tropical waters. There are sharks that live in extremely deep parts of the ocean, and also sharks that live in shallow water along coasts. Lots of sharks even travel over long distances, across oceans and between continents.

MORE ACTION-PACKED ADVENTURES COMING SOON!

Wow! That was an awesome adventure! We've checked out tons of animal hunters on land, sea, and sky. You've scoped out raptors, prowled around with big cats, and even took a bite out of sharks. But there are so many animals to discover! We'll see you next time for more exciting expeditions!

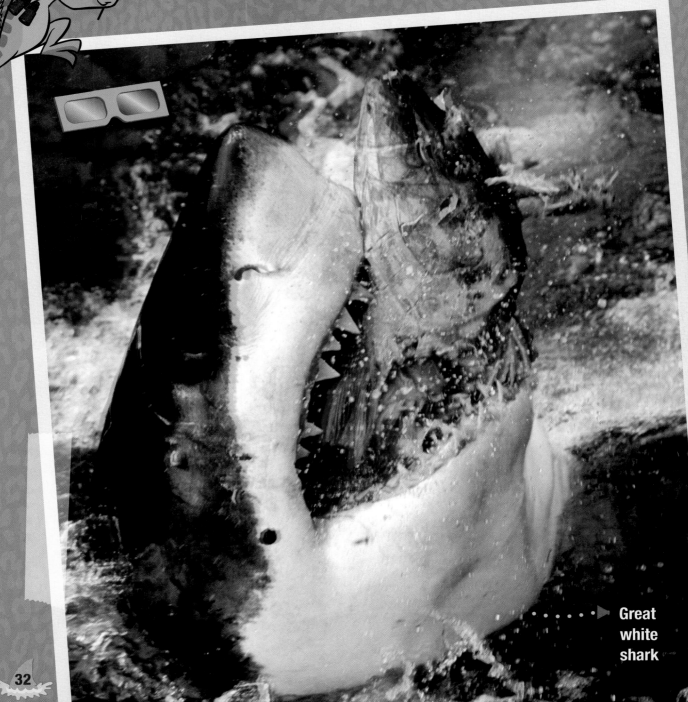

Great white shark